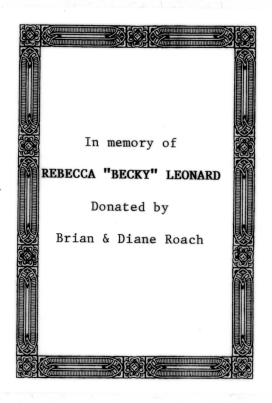

In memory of

REBECCA "BECKY" LEONARD

Donated by

Brian & Diane Roach

T

For information address Disney Editions, 114 Fifth Avenue, New York, New York 10011-5690.
Printed in the United States of America
First Edition
10 9 8 7 6 5 4 3 2 1

Library of Congress Cataloging-in-Publication Data on file.
ISBN: 0-7868-5321-2
Visit www.disneyeditions.com

THANK YOU, TEACHER

*Letters celebrating
extraordinary teachers*

Foreword by Michael D. Eisner

New York

Thank you to _____

_____

_____

_____

_____

_____

_____

_____

Signed

Contents

Foreword

The inspiration for *Disney's American Teacher Awards* can be found in the Oscar® telecast and the myriad other awards shows that have proliferated in recent years. All of these productions have one thing in common—they bestow honors on celebrities. In so doing, they reflect and reinforce the major role that celebrities have come to play in our society.

It's a curious term: "celebrity." It is based, of course, on the verb, "to celebrate." I have tremendous admiration for the people we usually think of as celebrities—actors, singers, directors, and so on. But I believe we are making a serious mistake if these are the only people we choose to celebrate. This is why Disney produces the annual American Teacher Awards. We feel it is wonderfully appropriate to mount an Oscar-style awards show to honor people who aren't found on the cover of *People* Magazine, but whose lives deserve to be celebrated across the land.

One of the pleasant surprises of the American Teacher Awards has been the discovery that the lives of our teacher celebrities are not only admirable but are every bit as dramatic as the latest Hollywood block-buster (often more so). These are dynamic, innovative, and creative people who have often worked against tremendous odds to inspire and motivate children of all ages and all circumstances. For them, the classroom is the ultimate stage where the ongoing stories of their students' education is played out. These are compelling stories that have no ending, since the students blessed with these devoted teachers find themselves imbued with a love of learning that lasts a lifetime.

This book relates some of these extraordinary stories. The teachers profiled in these pages may not be celebrities in the usual sense, but in a very real way they are the *ultimate* celebrities, leading lives for which we all should be grateful, lives that we should truly celebrate.

Michael D. Eisner

Inspiring Confidence

Teachers who help students
to build self-esteem and character

I thank you

    for how much patience you had with me

    for being the best teacher

    for pressuring me to do my work

    for getting me where I am now

    for giving me all of those compliments

    for making my school year so fun

    for making me feel that I am worth something

And most of all, I thank you for being more than a teacher to me—
you're also a true friend.

Andre Hernandez (age 15)
Former eighth-grade student of **JULIANNA EGGLESTON**
Syringa Middle School
Caldwell, Idaho

What makes Mrs. Dano special is her innate ability to access each child's needs and capabilities. She works with each child as if he or she is the only one in a class of sometimes as many as twenty-seven students. No child ever falls through the cracks if it's within her power. She customizes the curriculum to fit the children—presenting various options until each child finds what best suits him or her. As we all know, no two children are alike, so no two children learn alike. Knowing failure often leads to frustration, she constantly reminds her students that there is no learning without mistakes, and the only failure is not learning from your mistakes. She prides herself on helping each student develop and maintain a strong level of self-esteem, at an age where ego is extremely fragile.

My favorite story is about my own son. Micah was a very quiet and shy little boy. At my first parent-teacher conference, although he got great reviews with regard to his work, Mrs. Dano was concerned about Micah's shyness and self-esteem. After talking with her for a bit, I realized that Mrs. Dano had been doing her homework. She already was in touch with the gym teacher—sports are known to help foster self-esteem—working together, she assured me they would help Micah. Toward the end of the school year, Micah wrote an essay that was selected to be read in front of the entire school assembly. My husband and I, the proud parents that we are, attended with great apprehension. Would Micah get up and read his essay, or would he freeze? Sitting in the back of the auditorium with Mrs. Dano on the opposite side, Micah was called up. We waited with nervous anticipation, as he looked around for Mrs. Dano. Catching her eye, he began to read. Never missing a beat, he read to a wonderful round of applause. But, what Micah didn't see, and what I remember to this day, was Mrs. Dano raising her clenched fist in the air and letting out a loud "All right, Micah!" She turned to me, tears in her eyes, and I with tears in mine—and "thank you" didn't seem quite enough.

Andrea Tannenbaum, parent of Micah (age 16)
Former third-grade student of **LORI DANO**
Lido Elementary School
Lido Beach, New York

When an individual has the ability to inspire others, it is a gift. When that gift is bestowed upon children and generates an insatiable thirst for knowledge, this is a blessing. Irene Hines possesses that rare quality that encourages a child to actually desire the learning process, to search the halls of knowledge, and to open the doors to understanding and mastering the information and skills before them. There is an enthusiasm for teaching that shines forth so strongly from Ms. Hines that her students race to the challenge of learning with that same enthusiasm.

Every child who enters Ms. Hines's classroom feels like the most important star in the universe, capable of shining just as brightly as the most brilliant. The glow of excitement on my son's face as he returned home from school one winter day to tell me about his day is a memory that I will carry with me forever. It seems that as the day began, and the class entered their classroom, they found a sleeping Ms. Hines curled up on top of her desk in her pajamas and slippers with teddy bear and bedtime storybook in hand! Imagine the glee in that room when the children awakened their teacher and the joy with which she began an ordinary day for her class. Parents were always encouraged to join in classes to read to the class while imitating the characters they were reading about. School was never mundane and learning was not conveyed through uninspired routine for her students. Happiness abounded in this classroom, and the children were rewarded with the heart and soul of an astoundingly creative teacher with a passion for guiding young minds to new heights of learning. Some teachers just teach. Teachers like Ms. Hines live to convey knowledge. Some angels don't just touch the heart, they reach a child's mind. Ms. Hines is that kind of angel.

Donna Carroll, parent of Brian (age 11)
Former first-grade student of **IRENE HINES**
Brookside Elementary School
Westwood, New Jersey

★

The most important lesson I learned in Mrs. Campbell's class is this: regardless of your age, you are always a person who makes choices that will be uniquely yours forever; you don't just magically turn into a well-developed human being the day you turn twenty-one. Because of this lesson, I have been more careful about the decisions I have made, and, at the same time, I have enjoyed my life much more.

In my mind, Mrs. Campbell needs no award to prove that she is one of the greatest teachers alive. The proof lies in the lives of hundreds of well-developed individuals who, in prepubescent life, complained about having to diagram sentences, laughed at twelve-year-olds' pranks, and loved Mrs. Campbell.

Eliza Campbell (age 18)
Former sixth- to eighth-grade student of **LIBBY CAMPBELL**
North Iredell Middle School
Olin, North Carolina

★

Close your eyes; think back to your years in school. There's one teacher who stands out in your mind—she's far and away the most wonderful teacher you ever had. She made her subject come alive, she inspired you, she loved you, she fussed at you, and she pushed you to excellence. You wanted your homework to be perfect. You looked forward to her class all day. Her class was way too short (the clock must be wrong!). For my son Michael, this teacher is Ms. Richardson.

When I asked him what made Ms. Richardson special, he said, "Everything. I was seriously behind in Spanish, and she stayed after to help me; really, she taught me the seventh- and eighth-grade lessons simultaneously. She didn't just use the book. She made Spanish come alive. I still remember all of the zoo animals because of her silly stories. She decorated her room for *Cinco de Mayo* and *Dia de los Muertos*. She cooked tamales for us. She played music and told us how Hispanic families celebrate Christmas and New Year's. Oh, and she made us do that awful research paper IN SPANISH at the end of the year." (This is Spanish I; high schoolers do it in a year. Junior high spreads it over two years for a single high school credit. A research paper in Spanish, at this point, is pretty ambitious.)

My son, now a senior in high school, said to me, "Oh yeah. I still remember people grumbling about her famous paper. Everyone hated it. Some guy even had his mom call the principal and complain that it was too much work."

To which Mike replied, "Well, when I got to Spanish II in high school, the kids from Ms. Richardson's class were miles ahead of everyone else. The first marking period was a review for us." What a testament to her skill as a teacher. She had a struggling student, who was way behind, and in a single year taught him so much that he was ahead when he got to high school. I'm pretty impressed. I'm also impressed by the character she instilled in her students. She helped them to establish good study skills. She demanded excellence. And she wouldn't go easy on them because the president of the PTO complained that she gave too much homework.

My son was so enamored of Ms. Richardson that he insisted on coming to open house "in case you get lost and can't find her." Good thing—I almost missed her.

I wish for all children to have a Ms. Richardson. I wish for all children to have an adult apart from a parent who loves and cares for them. I wish for all children to have a model of excellence, character, and innovation.

Susan Strickland Canter, parent of Michael (age 17)
Former eighth-grade student of **WANDA RICHARDSON**
Kleb Intermediate School
Klein, Texas

I'm seventeen years old with severe Tourette's syndrome, ADHD, and obsessive-compulsive disorder. All these disorders make my life in school very difficult, academically as well as socially.

After being sheltered in a residential school for a few years, I wanted to come home, live with my parents and sisters, and face the "real world." My parents enrolled me in BOCES (special education) here in Goshen, because of small classes. Well, I wasn't prepared for "the real world" in BOCES and felt overwhelmed.

Enter Mrs. Carol Bierman—the most understanding and compassionate person I know. Mrs. Bierman gave me courage, and taught me to ignore all my "friends" that teased me. She always believed in me, even when I didn't believe in myself. Her constant words of encouragement helped me, especially on my rough days.

On those rough days, she would find me an empty classroom and sit and talk with me until I felt better and was ready to go back to my classroom and "face the music." Mrs. Bierman taught me the meaning of respect. If you show respect to her, she will have triple respect for you. I am happy to say that thanks to Mrs. Carol Bierman, I am now in a regular high school, very happy with my school, and I owe it to her for believing in me. She always said, "If you can believe it, you can achieve it." I'm determined to graduate next year with a high school diploma.

I owe a lot of love and thanks to Mrs. Bierman for all she has done for me and all the other lucky students, and wish she could be my teacher in Goshen High. Nevertheless, I know that she will always be my friend.

Idan Udalevich (age 17)
Former student of **CAROL BIERMAN**
Board of Cooperative Educational Services (BOCES)
Goshen, New York

Building a Haven

Teachers who create a safe environment

in which to learn

When Superman was laid low by kryptonite, at death's door, his life energy draining away, it was Lois Lane who came to his rescue. Removing the kryptonite, *she* saved *him*, and yet she then stepped back and let him be the hero.

My child is a superkid to me, and in today's society, different types of kryptonite abound: drugs, gangs, peer pressure, violence.

Kay Little guards and protects all of her students. She shields them with caring and love that they bask in. But we have also asked her to fulfill other, conflicting assignments. We ask her to embolden and encourage our children to explore learning and the world. But there are many aspects of the world I would not like my child to experience, not yet. So conflict is always there. We want them to find adventure, to go far and wide exploring freely, but we want to be able to bring them back home safe and unscarred.

Tackling this complex and conflicting assignment is the very strength of Mrs. Little. She has that rare ability to know how much is possible for these young minds and accept nothing less, to lovingly and firmly guide our children and yet release them at the very moment of discovery so that each child can claim the discovery as their own. My daughter Quinn's eyes show the pride she has, and that she knows I will have in each new insight she relates to me.

Mrs. Little takes photos all year and has a show at the end of the year for the parents, that the children accompany with a song. It is a song the class sings and signs in American Sign Language at the end of each day, a song that each parent learns from their child through constant repetition. One of the lines is, "How can anyone ever tell you, you are anything less than beautiful?" The show was a wild success last year. It was so touching that there were no dry eyes, except for those of the children. They sang and danced and showed off to their parents how much they had accomplished.

Jeff McLean, parent of Quinn (age 7)
First- and second-grade student of **KAY LITTLE**
Lindo Park School
Lakeside, California

★

I am not going to write about innovative teaching methods or the wonderful programs that Mrs. Good has created. What I will tell you about are the feelings that my child shares with me about her school day. My child comes home happy. She goes to school with a smile on her face. She wants to be *with* her teacher. My daughter knows she can learn anything, she knows anything worth achieving will take hard work, she knows she is valuable and has a tremendous amount to contribute to her class, her school, and her community. Mrs. Good works hard with her class to empower them. These students are strong! Strong in the belief that they can move mountains, if only because their teacher says they can.

True learning comes when a child is safe and valued. Mrs. Good told me that my daughter says to her "I don't understand what you are telling me. Can you say it in different words?" On the surface, this may not seem like much, but it says to me that my child really trusts her teacher. It is not any easier for a child to say she does not understand than it is for an adult. Too often, our children do not understand what is being told to them, and they do not feel safe enough to ask. Our teachers do not take the time to explain, in a variety of ways, until they really understand. Penny Good is extraordinary.

Wendy Klivans, parent of Sarah (age 8)
Second-grade student of **PENNY GOOD**
Peters Canyon Elementary School
Tustin, California

My son Nicholas was diagnosed at one and one-half years of age with autism. At age five, a crucial age in the development of autistic children, Nicholas was lucky enough to be a student of Anita Katz. She was, and continues to be our guardian angel. Nicholas is now thirteen years old. As his mother, I would like to write the following letter of recommendation on his behalf:

"Dear Mrs. Katz,

There is so much to thank you for, and so little space to do it in. I came to you as a child lost in his own world because I could not make sense of the confusion and turmoil around me. In your class, there were 'centers' that I went to; the math center, the reading center, etc. This provided the structure I so desperately needed. You know how hard transitions were. You gave me verbal and visual cues whenever a transition was to take place, each and every time, every day. You know how difficult it was for me to handle 'change.' Yet you built in small amounts of change throughout my day because you knew it was something that I needed to tolerate if I was to function in your world. You were the one constant force I could count on in my school day. You know the importance of imaginative play, a skill that comes so naturally to other children. You taught me how to play with cars and trucks and blocks and not just line them up. You taught me the social skills I needed in order to interact with the other students. I had friends in your class. I went to my first friend's birthday party.

"For children with communication disorders, communication between home and school is vital if progress is to be seen. You know the importance of this. You sent home a daily schedule of activities I was working on. It was filled with details and comments so that my mom could also work with me at home on these same things. This required a lot of time and effort on your part. Yet, you did this day after day, month after month. This provided me with the continuity that I needed in order to succeed. You took the time to call my mom periodically to see how things were going at home. You asked if there were problems or situations at home that my mom needed help with. You were always trying to learn as much as you could about autism and other communication disorders. You know about my mom's extensive knowledge of autism and were not afraid to ask her questions and advice when you needed help with something. You know how important it was for parents to have emotional support from other parents. You put my mom in touch with other parents in similar situations so that they could help each other.

"Thank you, Mrs. Katz, for always being there for my mom. You provided her with the emotional support she needed, especially during those crucial years. You gave her the strength and hope that she needed in order to help me. You were and continue to always be there for us, no matter what is asked of you. For this we will be forever grateful. . . ."

> *Elizabeth Cassese* for her son Nicholas (age 13)
> Student of **ANITA KATZ**
> P.S. 224 at P.S. 710
> New York, New York

★

My son, Michael, has cerebral palsy, which confines him to a wheelchair. He also has cortical visual impairment which makes his visual world changing and confusing. Because of these disabilities, no classroom could be found that was suitable for Michael. For more than a year, he had a home teacher while we searched for the right classroom. Then, one day, a year and a half ago, Michael's vision specialist called to tell me that she had located the perfect classroom and a remarkable teacher, Michael English.

Hopeful, but wary, I visited Mr. English's class. When I walked in, I immediately felt an atmosphere of warmth—the sense that I was in a home. As I walked around the room, I was impressed by the stimulating environment—walls filled with children's work, computers humming, a bubbling fish tank, a class library overflowing with books. I could feel the happiness of the children—the busy hum of a well-run class. I knew that this was where I wanted my son.

With trepidation, we asked if Mr. English would take Michael. "Sure!" he said cheerfully.

That "sure" was the start of Michael's miracle. Michael, who was so quiet, is blossoming in the presence of Mr. English's exuberant approach to learning. He no longer cries when we put him on the special school bus each morning. Math, which Michael had so detested, is now his favorite subject because "Mr. English makes counting fun." Michael's whining about what he thinks he can't do has no effect on Mr. English. Mr. English expects effort, not perfection. And Michael will now *try* to hold a pencil, will *try* to catch a ball, will *try* to push his wheelchair across the room, will *try* to focus on the letters of the alphabet—and success has sprung from these efforts.

The mutual respect that Mr. English fosters among the children is amazing. Michael now has friends, something that had eluded him for so long. When Michael first pushed his wheelchair straight instead of in circles, the class cheered. When he was home with chicken pox, the class called to say how much they missed him. When P.E. comes, the students vie for the chance to push Michael to the play area. A little boy who was so isolated is enjoying, for the first time, being a part of a group of children his age.

This kind of classroom, this kind of success, doesn't just happen. I have seen many classrooms, many fine teachers, but Mr. English is more than a very good teacher. He is a conductor. The success and harmony of his students are his music, and music fills his room. He pours his energy, his joy into making this beautiful music come from children others might hear as discordant notes: children like Michael, who don't "fit" into a regular classroom; the children that other, less giving, less gifted, less dedicated teachers would rather not have. With these children, Mr. English creates a symphony.

Lynn Todd, parent of Michael (age 7)
Student of **MICHAEL ENGLISH**
Joaquin Miller Elementary School
Burbank, California

You should see our classroom! Instead of the overhead lights on all the time, there are tons of lamps to give the class a homey feeling. There is also a big couch where we can read. Mr. Keller is a very talented piano player, and he also plays the violin. We even have a piano in our classroom that he plays for us sometimes!

I have learned SO much from Mr. Keller this year! He teaches us Latin roots, and eighth- or ninth-grade-level vocabulary words. I have learned so many words, I can talk like my uncle who uses HUGE words! Everyone in my class loves, I mean LOVES, my teacher. I am so lucky I get to have him for two years! I've had a lot of great teachers, but he is the best teacher I have EVER had! He REALLY deserves the American Teacher Award!

Lauren Cooper (age 11)
Fifth-grade student of **John Keller**
Eisenhower Elementary School
Warsaw, Indiana

Mrs. James taught both of my children. For one particular assignment, the children in my oldest son's first-grade class were given a paper that asked them to put an object in its proper place. The object was a dog bone, which was to be placed in the dog dish. My son put the bone in the trash can, and it was marked wrong. Mrs. James questioned my son as to why he chose the trash can. He remarked that it could have been a chicken bone, which would have hurt the dog. Mrs. James laughed, hugged him, and marked his answer correct. My son knew it was okay to think.

On one particular occasion, Mrs. James had the children singing "Silent Night" while walking to the library. My youngest son told her the children sounded so beautiful that he felt like crying. She smiled, hugged him, and they both shed a tear. He knew it was okay to feel.

Mrs. James has the ability to bring out the best in each child regardless of how different they are. She celebrates her students' intelligence and sensitivities. She encourages each and every little person to use his or her particular gifts. She is always positive, caring, and respectful.

Ann Bell, parent of Adam (age 21) and Jason (age 14)
Former first-grade students of **KATHY JAMES**
St. Joseph (Fullerton) School
Baltimore, Maryland

Randy Rosenblum is the art teacher in an extraordinary school of special-needs kids who are indeed fortunate to have her as their guide to the rewards of creativity.

Ms. Rosenblum is a highly creative person. Her tiny, cramped art room overflows not only with art materials, but also with everyday materials. It is her ability to see the world as infinite combinations of textures, colors, shapes, sounds, and smells, which help to expand these children's experience of the world—a world which often seems overwhelming and terrifying. For these children, everything in Ms. Rosenblum's world is an opportunity for learning.

But learning has a poignant dimension for these children. Ms. Rosenblum has the greater gift of teaching each of these children that they have self-worth—that they can give to others.

She truly believes in each of these children and from  that they have learned to value themselves. When my daughter came home and announced, "I'm an artist!" in a voice I had never heard before, I cried. Although she is not an artist in the classic sense, she believes she is. From the spirit of achievement my daughter has gained in Ms. Rosenblum's art room, I have been humbled. I, too, have learned.

For the past three years Ms. Rosenblum has organized an art show from which the proceeds of sales of student art go to programs for children in a local homeless shelter. In this one act alone, her students, to whom so many give so much, learn that they too can give, and that they can give from their ability to create. This demonstration of creating in order to give is itself an exceptional gift from Ms. Rosenblum to our children.

Pamela Wintle, parent of Elizabeth Griffin (age 14)
Student of **RANDY ROSENBLUM**
The Ivymount School
Rockville, Maryland

Respecting the World

Teachers who encourage students
to appreciate others and the world

Early in the year my daughter told me, "Miss Scott never uses a mad voice when kids are bad, she makes them mind with her eyes."

Miss Scott to me embodies what Disney represents, one who stimulates children to dare to dream, to create, to invent and not be afraid of failure, to believe in themselves regardless of their academic ability. She has the rare trait of drawing out the creativity in her students that we too often stifle, especially with our focus on grades.

She truly identifies the uniqueness in each individual and helps them to develop it. Often our daughter's papers include a personal note encouraging a character trait reflected in her writing.

Miss Scott has developed a love for literature in her class, using different means to allow the child to relate to the characters. Last week her class was reading *Pippi Longstocking*, and they went outside and became "thing finders" like Pippi. They then came in and made something with their "things" and wrote about their "invention." Our daughter came running home beaming with excitement over her accomplishment.

Years ago Miss Scott started each child's "special week" program. She has accomplished so much more than the obvious; her students learn how to handle authority during their week and respect it during those of their classmates. Each student writes thank-you letters to the

"special child" and their family for who they are and what they have shared. Our daughter read her packet of letters over and over, hugged it, and looked at me and said, "I just can't stop smiling." Miss Scott accomplished in a week what we as parents have spent years trying to develop.

Finally I share this with you from a child's perspective. One night as I knelt with my daughter during bedtime prayers she said, "Dear Lord, please help me to be just like Miss Scott when I grow up because I know that will make you happy." I couldn't agree with her more.

Nancy Snyder, parent of Christine (age 9)
Third-grade student of **JANENNE SCOTT**
Oakland Elementary School
Bloomington, Illinois

★

Even the most mundane tasks of any classroom are made into magic by dr. deb. The job list isn't just a list. It's a pair of overalls with the daily jobs appearing as pockets all over the overalls. The timer to announce that it's time to rotate groups for learning centers doesn't ding. It's a rooster and it crows. And the children just don't walk from one center to the other. They hum a theme song along the way. During the unit on space, it was the theme to *Star Wars*. And during the unit on the Wild West, they hummed the Roy Rogers–Dale Evans hit "Happy Trails to You." A walk down the corridor to lunch isn't a walk, it's a saddle-sore buckaroo's jaunt, or a Native American's quiet tiptoe in the forest.

dr. deb has not only created a visually stimulating classroom, she has created a haven in which the children are bonded to each other with real caring and sharing. They feel safe and nurtured. Their learning is risk-free. They teach each other. The mutual respect for each other has become a celebration of their differences in their learning styles and how they can help each other. Creativity and imagination have become the very soul of the collective class.

I want to go back to kindergarten again—but only if I can have dr. deb.

Cynthia Graubart, parent of Rachel (age 6)
Kindergarten student of **DR. DEB ROSENSTEIN**
The Davis Academy
Atlanta, Georgia

I'm writing this letter to commend my son Edward's fourth-grade teacher, Christina Robson.

I have never seen her without a smile on her face, a sparkle in her eye, and an encouraging word on her lips. But she also sets the limits, and never retreats. She demands from each child respect for his or her classmates, and for himself or herself. Then she goes about her business with enthusiasm and purpose. Immediately the children *know* she cares about them, that they *matter*, that there are *expectations* for them, and that their time in the classroom will be a *partnership* between themselves and the teacher in pursuit of those expectations.

Her classroom keeps pace with the world. She hammers home the fundamentals, to be sure, but the children are exposed to so much more, including environmental protection, current events, preservation of endangered species, space exploration, art and art history, geology, geography, multiple forms of literature, principles of electricity, and, of course, computer technology.

Two weeks ago, her class presented a most *exceptional* hour-long program on endangered animals, featuring written materials, drawings, and oral presentations (accompanied by Microsoft PowerPoint video) all prepared by the students themselves. They even wore plaster masks, fashioned over a period of several days, molded and painted to look like the faces of the animals on which they were reporting. At the end they sang, "This Land Is My Land," and the parents wept. The children were exemplary, self-assured, and self-disciplined. Most of them had not begun the year that way.

Edward Fensholt, parent of Edward (age 10)
Fourth-grade student of **CHRISTINA ROBSON**
Countryside Elementary School
Olathe, Kansas

Chris Morgan seems to have an uncommon concern for the future of his students. For example, he has taken the fifth-grade bully and taught him to take responsibility for his own actions. This year the boy has shown remarkable improvement and self-control. Dealing with students who are at a difficult age (eleven years old), Mr. Morgan has found the key to every child's self-confidence and joy of learning.

He teaches that each child is responsible for his or her actions and can achieve the highest standards if they try. I have overheard him tell his class before leaving for a field trip, "Be on your best behavior. You are representing yourself, your parents, and your grandparents." And that same day, I overheard the compliment "This is the best–behaved class we have ever seen." His messages about life and respect really sink in.

Amy Grambeau, parent of Michelle (age 11)
Fifth-grade student of **CHRIS MORGAN**
Wines Elementary School
Ann Arbor, Michigan

Three days ago, my energetic eleven-year-old daughter ran in from soccer practice yelling, "Mom, Mom, you need to write a letter about Mrs. Wise!" My daughter isn't pushy, nor is she impulsive or rude, but on this particular matter she seemed very enthusiastic.

"Okay," I told her. "You nominated Mrs. Wise. Tell me why you think she's imaginative and creative. Give me examples."

My daughter looked at me and replied, "Mom, she's NICE!"

My reply to that was, "If I'm going to write a letter about her, I have to put in teaching methods encouraging exploration and imagination. 'Nice' doesn't tell me anything."

Then she took the form out of my hand and pointed to the word "inspire." I received a lecture from an eleven-year-old that I will never forget:

"Mrs. Wise is nice. She's really nice. Not many people are nice, you know. People yell and scream, even teachers. When teachers yell and scream and get tense, all of us students get tense. Sometimes teachers really stress us out. They talk about grades and test scores. Mrs. Wise doesn't yell and scream.

"Remember when Mrs. Wise told you that if your child ever feels stressed out because of school, to call her?

"She teaches us manners and how to behave. You know, Mom, we all need to have good manners in school and some kids don't even know what good manners are! She teaches us how to be good people.

"Did you forget about when the whole class went to the nursing home? We read our stories and our poetry and our book reports to the old people there. They really like hearing our stuff! We even talked to them about our lives and school and they told us really neat stories. The whole class was polite and NICE because Mrs. Wise expected that. We knew how to smile and RESPECT them because that's what we've been taught in her class.

"When parents or others come into our class to help or share information, we have to write thank-you notes. We even have to check our spelling and grammar when we write them!

"You know what, Mom? No one argues with her about writing thank-you notes for stuff. I think everyone wants to be as nice as her.

"Teaching is more than just cramming stuff down our throats. Maybe if everyone taught the things Mrs. Wise did, no one would get shot in school, no one would put others down, no one would be rude, and everyone would learn to respect each other."

My daughter stopped and I took a breath. Maybe she's right. Maybe Mrs. Wise is teaching more than any other teacher in the entire world is. I like the ideas of reading book reports to senior citizens, editing thank-you notes, and volunteering time. I like the attitude of respect, good manners, and being NICE! Like a lot of parents, I work a lot and am not there as much as I'd like to be for my child. I check homework and monitor curriculum objectives. I know she's learning what she needs to. What I didn't realize until now was the most important lessons she was absorbing and taking to heart. Not only is she being INSPIRED in school, but she's being INSPIRED TO BE NICE!

Julie Sloane, parent of Krystina (age 11)
Sixth-grade student of **Pat Wise**
Lynn Haven Middle School
Virginia Beach, Virginia

Inventive Lessons
Teachers who engage students
with exciting ideas in the classroom

My daughter, Hannah, entered Mary Kiss's second-grade class in September 1997. By the end of the school year, Hannah had not only embraced the challenges asked of her, her exuberance for her second-grade year could be compared to the exhilaration one might feel after an enjoyable and activity-filled world tour.

Spelling lessons were transformed into units that incorporated rhythm and song; art projects were science projects in disguise (our breathtaking Christmas tree ornaments were made from crystallized borax); book reports—still a daunting task for second graders—became shoe box "floats" that instigated a class parade; reading became the theater; and field trips were more like expeditions. Through every academic subject, every project and every unexpected incident, Mary Kiss makes learning the goal without making it a chore.

Her school day normally begins with stretching and a quick jog out on the field. Miss Kiss is no armchair quarterback, either on the playground or in the classroom. She is always an active part of every event. Exuding enthusiasm at every turn, she lives her lessons so that her students learn *through* her, not just *from* her. Her balance of activities throughout the day always seems to fit the ups and downs of the collective classroom attention span. And even when the classroom is quiet, it is NEVER dull.

Susan Batt, parent of Hannah (age 10)
Former second-grade student of **Mary Kiss**
Jerabek Elementary School
San Diego, California

36

What makes the learning in Mrs. Allen's classroom interesting and exciting is the way she presents the lessons. Not only does she explain the lesson, but also, she shows us, lets us taste, and feel. For example, we have been learning about Ancient Greece and the gods. One day she wanted us to taste Greek foods. Thus, she served us wonderful dishes; we helped to cook them.

I have always enjoyed Mrs. Allen, whether it's when she goes head over heels for Mel Gibson, talking about a chat with Mickey Mouse in Disneyland, sighing over a bite of Hershey's chocolate, or just having one of those days. Whether it's humorous, nerve-racking, or heart-breaking, I'll never forget my teacher, Mrs. Allen.

By the way, it would be nice if Mrs. Allen could meet Mel Gibson, just so you know.

Tony Gonzalez (age 12)
Sixth-grade student of **MICHELLE ALLEN**
Reagan Magnet School
Odessa, Texas

I wish all first graders could spend that extraordinary time of their lives with a teacher like Thea Kay Tribble. She would make their world a better place; teaching them to love life, to love themselves, and to love learning. Mrs.

Tribble would be an excellent recipient of your award. She truly is an American treasure. I am proud and thankful that she touched my children's lives and mine.

Vicki Cooper, parent of Camille (age 6)
First-grade student of **THEA KAY TRIBBLE**
Oak Hill Academy
West Point, Mississippi

--- ⭐ ---

"**M**s. Barron this . . . Ms. Barron that . . . Ms. Barron said . . ." I promise that's all I've heard this year from my fifth-grade daughter, Kelsie. When I think of the amount of time Kelsie spends at school and the influences others have on her, I am so grateful for Ms. Barron's teaching with creativity, ability to compel an intense desire and excitement to learn, and her dedication to all of her students.

Whatever Ms. Barron teaches comes alive as a hands-on experience. Last month, Kelsie came home from school and said, "I am so mad today. You know how we are learning about the American Revolution? Ms. Barron divided the class up half into the British soldiers and half into the patriots. I'm a patriot, and every time I get up from my seat to get a drink or use my pencil, I have to give one of those British a piece of paper. Do you know how many pieces of paper I gave out today? About forty. And, Ms. Barron said she doesn't want to hear anyone

coming to her complaining about the taxes—like she's the King of England or something." For three days I heard about the unfairness of the paper tax. At the end of the third day, Kelsie said, "Mom, if I have to pay one more sheet of paper, I'm starting a revolution." On the fourth day, Ms. Barron directed retribution for the patriots' misery. The patriots stood on top of their desks, balled up their paper, and threw it onto the floor while the British picked it up. Kelsie said it was all worth it. The class also reenacted the Boston Massacre. Kelsie came home each day teaching me details of the Revolution I never knew.

The only problem with a teacher like Ms. Barron is now Kelsie knows what fantastic teaching feels like, and everything less will be just plain old school.

Michelle Barrow, parent of Kelsie (age 11)
Fifth-grade student of **MARY GIN BARRON**
Hailey Elementary School
Hailey, Idaho

———— ⭐ ————

So here I am, half awake, just concentrating on putting one foot in front of the other as I head down the hall to my locker. My backpack feels like a ton of bricks, intent on dragging me to the floor as I fumble with my combination. After I finally open my locker, I shove the pack inside and then rub my eyes and blink a couple of times. What day is today, I wonder? Tuesday? Wednesday? Suddenly I snap awake. Yes . . . it is Tuesday, and I have period three first . . . Language Arts with Ms. Baird!

My books don't seem to be such a tormenting weight anymore as I haul them out of the backpack. I shut my locker and then hurry into the classroom. I just wrote a piece that I think is something else, and I can hardly wait to share it with her. This excitement is what I get each and every time I walk into Ms. Baird's class.

When Ms. Baird sets a new thing on the overhead projector, we practically grip our seats with anticipation! We know that there isn't a boring lecture coming. A discussion will follow that clear sheet—one in which we can all chime in with raised hands to crack jokes and tell stories related to the topic. There we are, enjoying the lesson, and in enjoying it, remembering it. We are building more confidence in our skills with every second.

Jessica Johnson (age 14)
Eighth-grade student of **Susan Baird**
Ashland Elementary School
Ashland, Oregon

From the moment he received his "Welcome to first grade" letter, my son was as excited as I have ever seen him. This excitement lasted all year long as Mrs. Barclay, a remarkable and enthusiastic teacher, took a marginally confident boy and turned him into a reader, and author, a mathematician, and a "penguin expert." She instilled in him, and every other child in that class, such a love of learning and such respect for each other's learning styles and strengths that upper-grade teachers can pick out which children came from her classroom by their approach to their own learning.

Mrs. Barclay's classroom is one of joy and excitement where all are welcome and all ideas and questions are honored. She creates a learning environment where students work in cooperative groups, are taught to self-assess and become passionate assistants to one another. Parent involvement and communication is the norm; Mrs. Barclay sends home newsletters several times a week which include suggestions of activities to complement classroom instruction and themes. Her classroom is a print-rich environment, full of books in every learning center, with student work covering not just the classroom, but the corridors and any available bulletin board in the school.

What most amazes me about Mrs. Barclay is her ability and tenacity when it comes to the instruction of reading. Regardless of learning abilities, she firmly believes that every child can learn to read in first grade—and she makes sure they do. Her approach, using a featured "Author of the Month" and "Books on the Go" to supplement the reading program allows children to read what they are interested in and allows for flexibility in pacing. I marvel at the way she seems to be in three places at once—gliding effortlessly and knowingly from child to child, ready to offer encouragement or assistance to keep confidence levels high at all times. By the end of the first grade year, my son, and every other child in the room, was reading fluently, and constantly! My son now carries a book everywhere he goes. At their spring Author's Breakfast, every child presented and read his/her first "published book" complete to every detail, with copyright and a dedication.

Jeanne Perrin, parent of Alejandro Escobar (age 9)
Former first-grade student of **KERRI BARCLAY**
Cottage Street Elementary School
Sharon, Massachusetts

"**H**oney, your teacher called me today."

My fork froze in midair, dangling in front of my face as my stomach turned to ice.

"Oh?" I managed to force out in the most nonchalant voice I could muster.

"Mmm-hmm. He said that essay you handed in today—remember the one you've been working so hard on?—is one of the best pieces he's ever received from a student! Atta girl!"

With that, my jaw and my peas dropped to the floor.

Never, in all my experience as a student, had one of my teachers called home because I had done something *good*. Furthermore, I had never had an English instructor who believed I had so much talent. Mr. Burruto constantly challenged me to improve my language skills, to live up to my full potential. I resisted at first, my method of improvised, unedited writing was, by ninth grade, a comfortable rut. But he persisted, with more patience than I deserved, until I started putting real effort into my essays. My motivating thought while I was composing what won me the above-mentioned phone call was, *I'm going to knock his SOCKS off*. Mr. Burruto lit a fire under me that has never been extinguished.

Megan Potts (age 18)
Former eighth-grade student of **CHRISTOPHER BURRUTO**
Johanna Perrin Middle School
Fairport, New York

My daughter Katie cries on snow days. I would cry on snow days, too, if Mrs. Chris Arcangelo were my kindergarten teacher. While other kids hope for a day off from school at the first hint of snow, Katie asks me to drive over to the school in a blizzard, just in case Mrs. Arcangelo might be there. Sometimes she is. Her enthusiasm for teaching is matched only by her enthusiasm for learning—she is a teacher who soaks up experience like a sponge, then shares it generously with those around her, especially our children.

My daughter's school day flies by . . . from 8:15 A.M. to 2:40 P.M., she's caught up in the discovery of learning reading, math, religion, and science, guided and enriched by Chris Arcangelo's hands-on teaching methods. They not only read books . . . they create their own. Not only do they take field trips to see puppet shows . . . they write, produce, and act out their own. They nurture butterflies from tiny caterpillars to brilliant creatures, as they spread their own wings while learning about nature and life's mysteries.

> *Judy Burns,* parent of Katie (age 6)
> Kindergarten student of **Chris Arcangelo**
> St. Gregory's Early Childhood Center
> Clarks Summit, Pennsylvania

Imagine how thrilled I was—as a professional scientist—when Emilie Sullivan, the coolest science teacher in the world, entered the lives of my children. Now I have a teenage daughter who wants to be a biologist (not like her fusty old astrophysicist dad), volunteers to help in science classrooms, and likes to collect samples of everything currently or formerly alive and put them under her microscope. If all of our teachers were like this, the future of the world would look very bright indeed!

The rich display of ideas and exploration I witnessed upon visiting her middle-school classroom brought me back to my own roots and the sheer joy and playfulness of science. I was thrilled when Emilie Sullivan agreed to become a partner with our department at the University of Washington. For three years now, our university researchers have

learned from her energy, creative imagination, and exceptional talent at connecting with kids. At our first department open house this spring, we invited Emilie's classroom to present their project posters to our thousands of visitors alongside the research of our own undergraduates, doctoral students, and faculty. Chairs of other university science departments declared their astonishment and my heart filled with pride at the passion for knowledge in the work of these seventh graders. And I know that I only see one view of Emilie's multifaceted talents—her kids are not only solving crimes and the mysteries of the universe, they are also seeking cures for cancer. Certainly my fourteen-year-old daughter has started working on it—thanks to Emilie Sullivan.

Craig Hogan, parent of Aneila (age 14) and Patrick (age 16)
Former seventh-grade students of **Emilie Sullivan**
Kellogg Middle School, Shoreline School District
Seattle, Washington

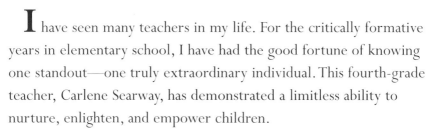

I have seen many teachers in my life. For the critically formative years in elementary school, I have had the good fortune of knowing one standout—one truly extraordinary individual. This fourth-grade teacher, Carlene Searway, has demonstrated a limitless ability to nurture, enlighten, and empower children.

It's been said that "a teacher opens the door, but it is the child that must walk through." I truly believe Carlene Searway not only opened the doorway, but has inspired, encouraged, and been the bright torch to light the way for my children as they passed from the safety and security of their childhood and elementary school experience and emerged into the much bigger world beyond. I can't imagine a teacher with better credentials, a teacher with more energy, enthusiasm, or love for her charges.

Paul Stauffer, parent of Ryan, Alison, and Jessica
Former fourth-grade students of **CARLENE SEARWAY**
Mary Silviera Elementary School
San Rafael, California

Giving 110%

Teachers who consistently go
above and beyond the call of duty

I am a green plant that hangs in the window of Mrs. Gangstad's first-grade classroom. I have been here all year and have seen everything that goes on in this very happy classroom. I watch Mrs. Gangstad come in early to gather inspiration for the day. I watch the children come and go and learn and grow. And, I watch Mrs. Gangstad stay late to perfect tomorrow's lessons and make telephone calls to parents.

Some of the most memorable moments for me: Peter sharing his collection of seventy-nine frogs, baking pumpkin pies, hatching baby chicks, singing patriotic songs for the whole school, making a real television commercial about recycling, touring an Indy 500 garage, sharing stories about pets, and going around the world in "hot air balloons" for our reading program.

But, I also see some things that most parents don't even know about. For instance, Mrs. Gangstad has made Christie's tummyaches disappear, taught Manuel how to understand  English, and made Max feel lucky to have two moms and two dads. Mrs. Gangstad has listened to Sandy talk and talk even though the children rarely hear her speak. Mrs. Gangstad has given Jasmine room to express her creativity and made Anna proud of her freckles. She has given Aron challenging books to read and made sure Andrew gets extra help in math. Mrs. Gangstad has taken Kyle to Dairy

Queen to celebrate good behavior. She has taught these children the importance of family and love.

Betsy Laskey, parent of Peter (age 6)
First-grade student of **DEBORAH GANGSTAD**
College Wood Elementary
Carmel, Indiana

I looked forward to being in David Baker's class because I learned, and was intrigued by the way the whole class learned. Somehow this man could broadcast on several different wavelengths at once, and my classmates were sure to pick up at least one. His excitement for what he taught was contagious. At once, he had absolute authority and the students' trust.

The best teachers have a passion for what they teach *and* a passion for their students. They aren't afraid to get involved in their kids' lives. David Baker is such a teacher.

David Baker pounded "above and beyond" into our heads. To do the assignment was good, but going above and beyond what was required was worth another letter grade or at least some extra credit. I competed with myself to reach new heights instead of waiting for my classmates.

I watch the beginning of one of his classes. He's

teaching about exponents. Soon he has the class begging me for the answers. Deftly he brings the attention back to the chalkboard where a volunteer is working out a problem. A curious girl raises her hand to ask what happens if there's a negative exponent and David Baker puts aside his lesson plan to teach what the class wants to learn. What does she think, he asks. He teaches by instructing the class in teaching itself.

Six years later, David Baker is still extraordinary. He doesn't expect more of his students than he asks of himself. Above and beyond begins with him. No one I know deserves this award more than he.

Diana Dameron (age 19)
Seventh- and eighth-grade student of **DAVID BAKER**
Mead Middle School
Mead, Colorado

I am the mother of three boys; the oldest is eighteen and the youngest is ten. I have to admit that my youngest son is a "wild child." Since my youngest first started kindergarten, he has struggled in every class, every grade, and with every teacher. He was always in trouble and getting into fights. He struggled with reading, math, music, and spent more time in the office than in his classes.

Last summer, the school posted which teachers the students would have. Just days before school was to start, I received a phone call to let me know that my son's teacher was changed to a new teacher at our school. My son was so excited because one of his best "show-off" buddies was in this class. I just cringed! I knew this would be the worst way that my son could start out the fourth grade.

So, I decided to call the teacher, Mrs. Kenney. I started out by saying that I love my son very much, but that I needed to let her know about him and his friend. I spoke with her for about twenty minutes and explained just how wild these two boys could be together. I told her how desperately my son needed a teacher who would not "baby" him— he must know the rules, and the consequences for breaking them must be real. I also told her that I would call the principal and ask that my son not be moved to that class for these very reasons. Mrs. Kenney's response was, "Thank you for the warning and your support, but I accept the challenge." This was the nicest, most positive way she could have handled this situation.

Just two days into the school year, Mrs. Kenney called me to say something very nice about my son. She assured me that she could find positive things to call home with so as to start reinforcing the positive rather than the negative, as every teacher had done before her.

She also gave him choices to help him change his behavior, such as when he chose to have his desk away from other students so he wouldn't be tempted to talk. This helped facilitate more good behavior for her to call home about.

There was also one day when he and another boy just couldn't sit still in their seats. She gave them a challenge. She told them that since they were so squirmy, she wanted to see if they could stay inside for recess and wiggle every part of their bodies for the entire time without stopping. And they did. Not only did she say it was the funniest thing she ever saw, but that they were exhausted and very well behaved for the rest of the day.

I believe the special gift this lady has to dig deep inside a student, not only to find the positive, but also undo the negative that has been reinforced by previous teachers is the greatest gift my son could ever receive. I will forever be grateful for the learning opportunities Mrs. Kenney has opened up for my son.

> *Sherry Bond*, parent of Eric (age 10)
> Fourth-grade student of **RUTH KENNEY**
> Terrace Park Elementary School
> Mountlake Terrace, Washington

★

My daughter will take with her many wonderful memories of kindergarten, lots of which have been preserved in a scrapbook lovingly prepared by her teacher. I will also have many fond memories and will always remember this profoundly talented teacher who gave my child such an excellent start. I will always remember her enthusiasm, dedication, and how much she acknowleged and supported my role as my child's educator. I will remember all the times I saw her at school late at night. I will remember writing this letter and feeling as though my words were inadequate to accurately convey what a gifted educator this woman is. To meet her, or to meet her students, speaks volumes about her ability; much more than I can express here. My hope is that she will always have the administrative and financial resources to support her creative methods of instruction so that she may continue to raise the bar of excellence in education and make a difference in a great many more lives.

Shannon Murray-Corsale, parent of Seana Corsale (age 6)
Kindergarten student of **NANCY VASILENKO**
Westbrook Elementary School
West Milford, New Jersey

Wonder of Learning

Teachers whose enthusiasm

for life and learning is contagious

Days in Mr. Coccarelli's class were unpredictable and never boring. He was never satisfied with just telling us information. He wanted us to ask questions and then discover the answers in the process. When we did, he was just as excited about what we

learned as we were. In his class we would walk to Food Lion and average food prices. We went on camping trips to study nature, and he had us balancing checkbooks at the ripe old age of ten. If you came to Magellan, you would recognize Mr. C. before you even saw him by his constant merry whistle or outbreak of song. Occasionally, you could find him waltzing down the halls with one of the other teachers. But don't get the impression that people don't take him seriously. I think because we respect him so much, it hurts us to disappoint him.

It may sound to you like Mr. Coccarelli is some kind of fairy-tale teacher, and in a way he is. Mr. Coccarelli is like no one you have ever met. His passion for life, learning, and teaching is what made every school day fly by. Whether he wins this award or not, this fact still remains: I will go on to high school and graduate from college and who knows what beyond that, but I will always and forever treasure the gift he has so eagerly given to me. He has shown me that life is *wonderful* and spilling over with opportunity, but the important thing is to keep your eyes open for it.

Holly Bryce (age 15)
Former fourth-grade student of **GEORGE COCCARELLI**
Magellan Charter School
Raleigh, North Carolina

Mrs. Wright's love of reading, writing, and storytelling accompanied by her spirit and openness touches her students every day. During class lectures, you can hear in her voice and see on her face a true love for her profession. Every day my fifth-grade year my classmates and I took a new adventure, traveling through literature, early America, and within a plant cell.

Never has there been a group of children more thrilled to hear rain pounding on the roof. Those raindrops were like sweet music to our ten-year-old ears. At recess the blinds would shut with a snap, the lights would be dimmed, and Mrs. Wright would take her place upon the stool at the front of the classroom. I can vividly remember the shiver of excitement that seemed to course through the entire room as her voice melodically rose and fell, a story unfolding before us. Whether a ghost story of her own creation or a tale from her past, Mrs. Wright never failed to delight us with her ability to bring words to life. She gave us that gift during a class assignment to write our own story, some of us presenting for a group of younger students. The assignment was just the first of many that taught us to find our own voice, though small at the time, we knew we could make a loud statement, a statement that shouted to the world, "Listen up! I've got something to say!"

Carla Hickman (age 16)
Former fifth-grade student of **BETTY WRIGHT**
Harrison Elementary School
Harrison, Tennessee

When Mrs. Campbell taught the Middle Ages, every day in school was an adventure. One day we were participating as a character in a Viking "Althyng," or trial, the next we were writing Skaldic poetry, or making medieval jewelry, or visiting the National Cathedral. We acted in Shakespeare's *A Midsummer Night's Dream* and did not change the words because Mrs. Campbell knew that we were capable of understanding them. We learned what the words to "Ring Around the Rosy" meant to those who lived during the days of the Black Plague, dancing around the room as we had when we were younger, but with a new, morbid understanding. She taught each one of us how to sew and make a tunic, and when we were finished we understood what it was like to have pride in our own work. We then wore the tunics to a Medieval fair and feast that we had planned. At the fair, we told fortunes, wrote in calligraphy, tried on chain-mail suits, watched knights duel, and rode in the "death car" when we were struck by the Bubonic Plague. To this day, I remember more about Gothic architecture and the Crusades than I do about geometry and ninth-grade English. Mrs. Campbell is a great teacher because she makes her students a part of the lesson; we did not learn history, we lived it.

Molly Elgin (age 17)
Former sixth-grade student of **WENDY CAMPBELL**
Canterbury Wood Elementary School
Annandale, Virginia

Whether we were playing an exciting game of "Around the World" to practice our math facts, a challenging game of *Jeopardy!* to review for our history test, or just listening to Mrs. Batdorf's soothing voice as she read a Judy Blume story, we were constantly learning. However, it did not seem like learning to us third graders, because we were having fun and enjoying the creative ideas of our teacher. We also delighted in moments of playful fun, like when she would reward us with her version of a lottery draw, or when the class would celebrate together for the holidays.

I learned so much from observing my third-grade teacher that year.

Most importantly, I learned how to set goals for myself. Sitting in my desk one afternoon, I set my ultimate goal, that one day I would become a teacher just like Mrs. Batdorf. She inspired me to want to touch the lives of others and make a difference in the world. The impact that Mrs. Batdorf made on me, as well as many of her other students, by her commitment and dedication to her profession, made me realize that I could do the same thing. I want to give to others the special gift that Mrs. Batdorf gave to me, the excitement of an education. Mrs. Batdorf has always encouraged her students to work up to their fullest potential, and explore new ideas each day. She makes learning an enthralling experience for everyone in her classroom.

Morgan Vance (age 18)
Former third-grade student of **SUSAN BATDORF**
Lyons Elementary School
Lyons, Ohio

———— ⭐ ————

Your love for reading and your desire to share it with children has been evident for the thirteen years that my three boys have experienced the loving arms of "Miss Shirley." No person tells a story better than you do, Miss Shirley. It is so powerful to watch wide-eyed children hang on every word as you imitate characters or act out parts of the story. Probably your best character, though, is the Easter Bunny. Each year when you pull that costume out of storage and hop down the "Bunny Trail," there are great debates about whether it really is Miss Shirley or the real thing!

Susan Lawhon, parent of Joshua, Paul, and Will
Former preschool students of **SHIRLEY PORTER**
Collierville United Methodist Preschool
Collierville, Tennessee

I took many journeys in Mrs. Greenstein's fourth-grade class and became more than a traveler. I also became an observer, and inventor, an astronaut, a detective, and astronomer, a writer, an artist, a scientist, a public speaker, and a devoted student, all while learning lessons I continue to use today in the seventh grade and will undoubtedly use in the many tomorrows to come. She opened my eyes to a world of exploration and taught me the skills I would need to continue investigating throughout my life.

Since leaving her class, I've often thought about how Mrs. Greenstein has improved my life. She instilled in me the joy of learning, and the desire to explore beyond the obvious. She taught me to believe in myself and to follow my love for science. It is because of her I attended space camp in the summer of fourth grade, and have been accepted into a special program at The Goddard Space Center this summer.

She showed me the stars and helped me reach for them. In my mind there is no one more deserving of Disney's American Teachers Award.

Sara Bloom Leeds (age 14)
Former fourth-grade student of **IRENE GREENSTEIN**
Lafayette Mills School
Manalapan, New Jersey

Kathy Dauscher teaches in a field of fireflies. It is an imaginary field, but to her students, it is a very real place. I have had the pleasure of working with Mrs. Dauscher over the past nineteen years, first as a student in her class, and then returning as a guest artist in her classroom. Kathy's ability to extend the threshold of the childhood imagination well beyond its allotted years is her true gift, and it shines through in everything she does.

Simply to visit her classroom stirs the imagination. Dragons swoop down from the ceiling. In one corner, a haiku garden studded with butterflies refreshes the mind; in another a terrarium teeming with living mysteries invites investigation. And everywhere there are books. She encourages her children to write using their own imaginations, to draw, and to create as part of the daily educational process. Even the sciences are enlivened with puppet shows, debates about nutrition, and artistic renderings of endangered species.

I have enjoyed her willingness to invite guest speakers to pepper the minds of her students with stories of faraway lands and varied

occupations. I have watched fourth graders, curious with anticipation as they are blindfolded by poets to listen to rain sticks, humpback whale songs, and the sounds of the orbiting planets. None of these experiences would be fruitful, however, without the readiness created by daily classroom discipline. They are good at listening because they practice listening; they write well because they write! write! write! And they are good scientists because their minds are free to explore many sides of the same problem.

When I say that Kathy Dauscher teaches in a field of fireflies, I am speaking of the luminous ideas that spark and swirl up from her students' fertile minds. Like any adventurer on a summer night, she knows the trick is to gather these tiny flames into a lamp by which to see the road ahead. In a world often darkened by ignorance and confusion, her students' lamps are brightly lit.

Mark Wonsidler (age 29)
Former fourth-grade student of **KATHY DAUSCHER**
Harry S Truman Elementary School
Allentown, Pennsylvania